The Art of Inspiration: Lead Your Best Story

Also by Justina Chen

North of Beautiful

Nothing but the Truth (and a few white lies)

Girl Overboard

Return to Me

A Blind Spot for Boys

The Patch

the art of
Inspiration

Lead Your Best **Story**

justina**chen**

Sparkline :: Story

Seattle, Washington

Library of Congress Cataloging-in-Publication Data

Chen, Justina Y.

The Art of Inspiration: Lead Your Best Story / Justina Chen.

1st ed. p. cm.

ISBN-13: 978-0988717411

ISBN-10: 0988717417

1. Leadership.

Printed in the United States of America

Designed by Robert Coronado

www.justinachen.com

To leaders, executives, and change agents:

storytellers all

"Make no little plans; they have no magic to stir men's blood ... Make big plans, aim high in hope and work."

—*Daniel Burnham, American architect & city planner*

Corollary for leaders

"Tell good stories; they have magic to stir people's blood. Lead your best story, aim high in hope and heart."

An Open Letter to Leaders, Changemakers, and Powers That Be

Your job is more than CEO, president, executive director, head honcho. You are more than a business strategist, statesperson, brand ambassador.

Arguably, your most important role is Chief Inspiration Officer.[1]

Whether you are rolling out a daring strategy, tackling a complex global issue, launching a long-awaited product, rallying employee morale, or hosting an all-hands meeting, you need to communicate with much more than clarity. You need to communicate with conviction and credibility. You need to communicate that you are a leader worth following. You need to stir your team, organization, volunteers, and donors to action. You need to inspire every one of your constituents to give the best of themselves to the organization's mission, strategy, product launch, campaign kickoff.

Let's take a quick assessment of your Inspiration Quotient:

- Are you a highly respected, oft-quoted, influential thought leader in your sphere?

- Are you inspiring and engaging a team so they're moving forward and acting?

- Can you command a stage? Rivet an audience so that they can quote you weeks and months after your speech?

- Can you communicate in a way that is both authentic and authoritative? Conversational and credible? Down-to-earth and decisive?

- Are you using your own personal stories to teach about successes and failures? Unify a team? Build your own credibility?

- Most importantly, do you communicate like the truly great leader you're meant to be?

[1] If I were coaching you, I'd say, "Please read that last sentence again. Aloud, complete with pauses and emphasis as if you were onstage. Oh, and make it personal: 'My MOST important role is... <Pause> Chief. <Pause> INSPIRATION. <Pause> Officer.'"

So. How'd you do?

As a leader, if you want to turn a business plan into inspired purpose, unite an organization, and captivate customers, you need to tell a story. If you want to be a leader who people faithfully and eagerly follow, you must tell a story. And not just any story, but a spellbinding, TED-worthy story. The stories that are most inspirational are authentic. And those are the ones that come straight out of you.

Study after study shows that storytelling is the most effective tool leaders have to drive impact. To teach about successes and failures. To unify a team with a shared purpose.

Study after study shows that truly great leaders are mission focused, and that inspirational leadership is the key to their success. It is the reason Dr. Howard Gardner wrote in *Leading Minds: An Anatomy of Leadership,* "Stories are the most important tool in a leader's toolkit."

All of this means that you as a leader need to be the Chief Inspiration Officer, not just of your organization, but of your industry or community-issue area. This is especially true if you are looking for a step-function jump in your career, if you want to be seen as a visionary, or if you truly want your cause, campaign, or product to succeed. YOU need to touch people at their deepest levels. YOU need to stir in them a deep sense of belonging and caring. And most of all, YOU need to master the Art of Inspiration. And you do that first by getting real onstage and sharing three types of stories: your organization's heritage and quest, your personal story, and your thought leadership.

For the last five years, I've coached leaders, prepping them for some of the biggest and highest-stakes world stages. These leaders have spanned presidents at Microsoft, and executives at major nonprofits and startups. They have commanded topics as diverse as financial literacy and cloud computing. Morale and malaria. Future-proofing global corporations and global health. Regardless of their subjects, they all share one common and constant refrain in the feedback for their speeches: Inspirational.

As in:

"Real, honest, and touching. Inspirational!"

"I walked away feeling proud! Inspired!"

"You walked up as an HR manager. You walked off as a Business Leader. Inspirational!"

Now, I want to share with you these storytelling secrets that have done much more than secure these executives higher speaker scores. Every one of the leaders I've coached has used these very storytelling secrets onstage to catalyze their leadership offstage. How? They shared their story—the Defining Moment that shaped who they are, what they believe in, and why they lead the way they do. They paid homage to their organization's Heritage and Quest. And they advanced their own, provocative and insightful Thought Leadership.

So embrace your role as Chief Inspiration Officer, and get personal, passionate, and provocative. When you do, you will deliver the shiver with a story that will establish you as a leader to follow.

Justina Chen
March, 2016

Prologue

January, 2010

EXT. LAS VEGAS STRIP - DAY

Thirty minutes after Robbie Bach, president of Microsoft Entertainment & Devices, leaves the stage after keynoting CES, the most influential computer industry trade show at the time, the communications team piles into a glossy, black stretch limo. No one has eaten more than a couple of handfuls of M&Ms back in the green room. JB Williams, general manager of Corporate Communications for Microsoft, leans toward the speechwriter with his phone.

                    JB
You've got to read this!

The speechwriter, exhausted from power-writing twenty-three versions of the keynote, cracks her eyes open, then squints, blinded, at the cell phone screen. She shrugs. Then JB, turning the phone back to himself, reads aloud:

                    JB
"Old white guys in suits shouldn't sound this good. Inspirational!" Best. Tweet. Ever.

Seven months earlier

Fourteen years after I left Microsoft to pursue my passion—writing young adult novels to shepherd girls to adulthood—I found myself the unwitting star of a midlife cliché. Soon after, I contacted my mentor, Pete Higgins, a former president of Microsoft, for wisdom. He took one look at fifteen-pounds lighter me and said, "You can't sit home all day, writing long, sad books in your pajamas. You need people. Get a job for a year." So I listened to him and forced myself back into the corporate world.

As it happened, Robbie Bach, my former boss and group product manager for Microsoft Office, was now the president of Microsoft Entertainment & Devices. A number of people had helped Robbie over the years with his speeches, but Robbie himself wanted to invigorate his communications with storytelling worthy of an entertainment company. He was intrigued about having me, a novelist with a marketing and PR background, spearhead storytelling. The only problem was, of course, I'd never written a single keynote before. Sure, I'd given speeches at countless high schools, colleges, libraries, and conferences on my book tours. But an industry keynote before thousands of the most cynical of press and most influential of customers? Keynotes to 40,000 employees at sports arenas complete with rock music, laser lights, and PowerPoints broadcast on screens that were three stories tall?

Pretty much never.

A little daunted, I did what novelists do. I started with a hero.

An excerpt from my take-a-chance-on-me letter

Dear Robbie,

I took the liberty of reviewing Steve Ballmer's keynote and demo at Mobile World Congress—and then contrasted that talk with Steve Jobs' launch of the iPhone. I was so dismayed by some of the missed messaging opportunities, I actually rewrote part of Ballmer's speech.

Here are a few thoughts about how you can use novel-writing precepts to strengthen your speeches:

Show, don't tell.

- *Ballmer tells us:* "More than anything, consumers want experiences that extend seamlessly across their home and work lives. They want to be able to connect only to the people and information that are important to them, from the PC or the phone, or directly to the web."

- *Instead, show us* with specific yet universal examples. "More than anything, Mom wants to snap pictures of her daughter's Famous Person presentation and send it to Grandma a thousand miles away. During the lull between Mother Teresa and Ghandi, she surreptitiously checks messages from work..."

Employ rhetoric to sound presidential and build to an emotional peak.

- *Ballmer tells us:* "becomes richer, more pervasive, and more universally useful."

- *Instead, try this:* "become more robust, more universal, MORE useful."

Hook your audience at the beginning; end with a bang.

- *Ballmer ends with:* "I want to leave people, however, with an upbeat message: no matter what goes on in the economy over the next few years, I guarantee you that technology and innovation are on a forward, upward and exciting curve, of which we are all glad to be a part."

- *Instead, try this:* "In history—whether in the Industrial Revolution or the Great Depression—it was technology and innovation that created change. Created opportunity. Created growth. The technology and innovation nurtured here in this conference, guided by my peers who I'm proud to speak with on the following panel, created by amazing brain power back in Redmond and you in this very room. We are on a forward, upward, and onward curve. Let's take the world on this ride with us."

Just my thoughts!
Tina

I got the job.

Even so, a few weeks into my new stint in executive communications, the corporate miasma threatened to suffocate me. Rounds of reviews with legal and finance desiccated the speeches of their juicy details. Well-intentioned marketers demanded that their focus-group tested messages be inserted word-for-word into the scripts. My manager wanted to know why it wasn't enough to throw bullets into PowerPoints and move on to the rest of the dozens of speeches that the president needed to give.

And so I succumbed to the peer pressure of corporate jargon and coma by PowerPoint. I slapped together a few slides, pockmarked them with bullets, and called it good enough.

Then came The Meeting. Robbie stared at me, still and silent, across the table in his corner office. This, alone, was alarming since Robbie is in perpetual motion: golf club in hand while on a conference call, pacing his office while thinking, man-striding across campus for a long day of back-to-back-to-back meetings.

"This is…" he sighed, eyes unwavering. "Well, boring."

Boring. That is the one-word death knell to novelists, particularly young adult novelists who know that the key to a teen's heart and attention is forward-propelling plot and breathless pacing.

Robbie placed the latest speech on the round conference table. The script was untouched, not even a single redline in the margin. And this was a president who edited down to periods and commas. He said, "And I sound like a marketing brochure."

Actually, I admitted to myself, what Robbie sounded like was an audio book for a marketing brochure, but this was what the company wanted. I said as much.

"Tina," he said, lowering his gaze, "I hired you for your words. Nobody else's."

"No," I said with the pent-up frustration of a word-bound writer as I glared at the do-not-resuscitate-for-good-reason document of boredom, "you hired me to tell stories."

To tell stories.

Those words rippled in seismic waves in Robbie's office, as he waited for my epiphany. He hadn't hired me to project-manage press releases or chase down missing cell phones held hostage in customs when we needed them for the Board of Directors meeting the next day. He hadn't hired me to review briefing documents for press interviews on his multi-country international trips. And he certainly didn't hire me to throw bullets onto PowerPoints and call that a speech.

I sat back in my chair, stunned.

From that moment on, the stories I found and Robbie told changed the tenor of his communications. He was connecting to his audiences of 40,000 employees who filled Safeco Field just as he was connecting to the mommy bloggers, the mainstream press, and his direct reports. More than that, the press was quoting him verbatim. His leadership team was citing him in their own all-hands meetings. His employees were flooding his inbox with messages about how proud they were to work in his division. He was managing the same business, battling the same competitors, and wrestling the same technical challenges. The only difference was that he was now harnessing the full power of storytelling. He told stories that shaped his leadership and illustrated his character. Stories that underscored his message so that people didn't just understand his vision; they engaged so much that his vision became their mission.

I have captured our most effective storytelling techniques in *The Art of Inspiration* for you. I deliberately wrote this book to be a short, concise guide to the craft of storytelling specifically for leaders. This is the curriculum that

I use to coach storytellers from AT&T to the Federal Reserve Bank and The Rockefeller Foundation. This is the same approach I continue to use with upstart leaders, whether they're running Fortune 10 corporations, nascent startups, or changemaking non-profit organizations.

Part One covers WHY storytelling is essential for leaders. In fact, the most common—and saddest— question that I receive whenever I speak at communications conferences: "How can I convince my leaders that they need to do storytelling?" This section reviews the quantitative research—in neuroscience and leadership—that underscores the need for leaders to be master storytellers.

Part Two describes the main "genres," or categories, of corporate storytelling that leaders must share. Specifically, the Heritage story that sets forth the genesis of the organization. The Defining Moment story, featuring the leaders and other change-makers within the organization. And the One Big Idea, or thought leadership story, that advances a unique and provocative worldview.

Part Three reviews storycraft. Specifically, I'll share a few of the most effective narrative tools that my executives have employed onstage. These are the very tools you can use immediately to sound more leaderly and inspire your corner of the world.

"When (Steve Jobs) got up in front of an audience to introduce a new product, he understood that he would communicate more effectively if he put forward a narrative, and anyone who ever saw him do it could tell you that he gave extraordinary and carefully crafted performances."

—*Ed Catmull, President of Pixar and author of Creativity, Inc.*

CONTENTS

Top 10 Traits of Extraordinary Leaders

1. **Real**: Extraordinary leaders strategically show vulnerability, which humanizes them and makes them authentic.

2. **Gritty**: Extraordinary leaders have intense personal fortitude to do whatever it takes to create a great outcome, enduring the hardest of obstacles.

3. **Self-aware**: Extraordinary leaders have a special knack for knowing their own weaknesses.

4. **Mission-driven**: Extraordinary leaders throw themselves into causes greater than themselves.

5. **Team-focused**: Extraordinary leaders think and talk in "we" not "I."

6. **Humble**: Extraordinary leaders know how the sometimes-traumatic hardships in their lives have shaped them and their leadership.

7. **Simplifiers**: Extraordinary leaders reduce complexity and frame the challenges their company, customers, and industry face in easy-to-understand terms.

8. **Dilemma flippers**: Extraordinary leaders spot opportunities where others see only problems.

9. **Growth-centric**: Extraordinary leaders are learners, viewing failures as education so mistakes are made once.

10. **Inspirational**: Extraordinary leaders communicate a compelling image of the future.

The Big Question

Do you exhibit these traits when you take the stage? Attend a meeting? Converse in the halls?

A Quick Quiz

How are YOU showing up as a leader?

- ☐ What are the traits of the right leader needed for your particular business right now?

- ☐ Are you showing up with those traits? Specifically, what stories do you share that demonstrate those traits?

- ☐ Are you coming across as authentic?

- ☐ Do people know just how gritty you are?

- ☐ Are you maximizing your onstage opportunities to drive home the importance of your organization's bigger quest?

- ☐ Are you seen as mission-focused?

- ☐ What stories are you sharing that TEACH about successes and failures? SIMPLIFY complexity? UNIFY a team with a shared purpose? BUILD your credibility?

- ☐ How are you revealing who you are at your core to create trust? To establish your credibility? To prove that you are the right leader for this moment?

"Why ... do most high-level executives struggle to communicate, let alone inspire? Too often, they get lost in the muddle of corporate communication. Instead, to motivate people, leaders must engage their emotions. And the key to people's hearts is story."

—*Rich Karlgaard, The Soft Edge*

PART ONE:

The Power of Story

Overview

Name a conference, any conference, where I have spoken to communications experts, and the top question I field is some variation of this: "How do I convince my executive that storytelling is important?" That usually opens the floodgates of frustration from the rest of the audience: "Yeah, how do I let my execs know that bullets and data aren't working?" And inevitably, the ad hoc therapy session ends with a final lament: "My executive just doesn't believe in storytelling."

So, my leader, why storytelling?

Just look at neuroscience research and how people remember information. Add to that the insistent drumbeat of leadership research, echoed by study after study: If you want to lead, you must be authentic. How can you be authentic if not through storytelling?

As Dr. Howard Gardner of Harvard says, "Stories are the most powerful tool in a leader's toolkit."

All of this means: Leaders today need to be exquisite storytellers who connect so powerfully with audiences that their listeners themselves become ambassadors, retelling the stories to others.

Why Tell Stories?

Rich Karlgaard, Publisher of *Forbes* magazine, wrote in *The Soft Edge:* "(I)f you want to get anything done in an organization, you need to know how to use story to motivate people."

Leaders, I'd add a few corollaries to that. Here are the top five reasons why you must tell stories.

Top 5 Reasons You Must Tell Stories

If you want to create change, you need to tell a compelling story.

If you want to control the message, you should to tell a tweet-worthy story.

If you want people to remember your message, you'd better tell a riveting story.

If you want people to believe in you as a leader, you have to tell your own story.

And if you want people to be more than loyal, but in love with your product, service, organization, or brand, you must tell a story.

ONE: Win people's hearts, and you win their minds and their feet.

The right stories will build trust, enthusiasm, and respect for your vision and strategy. No matter how hard or challenging the project or task you're asking people to take with you, they will throw themselves—hour after hour, sacrifice upon sacrifice—if they believe in the quest with utter conviction in their hearts. With the right story, you can connect both yourself and your audience to a mission much greater than yourselves. You can transmit your values—and the values of your organization. You can unite constituents behind your mission.

Let's take a trip through history just to glimpse at the power of a story that won people's hearts. Over fifty years ago, a quarter of a million people descended on Washington, D.C. to hear Dr. Martin Luther King, Jr.

Think about that. 250,000 people gathered together before Twitter. Before Tumblr. And before texting. They knew where and when to gather. And they gathered because they wanted to hear, as Simon Sinek pointed out aptly in his TED talk, Dr. King's dream, not his plan.

That one sixteen-minute speech energized the Civil Rights Movement and inspired an entire nation to join a quest for racial equity. Together, that groundswell of civic support turned one leader's dream into a plan. And that plan into action.

Magical stories have the power to win hearts, minds, and feet. They can drive people from seat to street. What's more, a story actually gains power in the retelling. As Wendy Levy, Executive Director of the National Alliance for Media Arts and Culture said at a Rockefeller Foundation convening on storytelling, "There is no power to the Like." No, the power lies completely in the Share.

What stories can leaders tell that are juicy enough, provocative enough, and powerful enough to warrant a Share? And are you, as our leaders—the ones who have the pulpit of the stage and press tours—telling stories that are so compelling, the audiences feel as if they can't wait to share it with others?

TWO: Good stories amplify your message. Great stories control your message.

The right story controls a message because it rivets the audience. It propels them to take note—literally. Just watch the verbatim quotes captured and transmitted through tweets during a keynote strategically architected with great stories.

I discovered this truth after the first major external-facing speech I wrote for Robbie Bach, then the President of Microsoft Entertainment & Devices. We were ready to launch the holiday lineup of products, including the game Halo. Our events team had created a special Open House for 150 of the most influential press. We knew we had to wow this jaded audience.

Robbie said to me, "I really want people to know about the personal passion behind our products." So I went in search of that story and found it through one of my division's intellectual-property lawyers. (Note: when you're story scouting, always chat with your company's IP lawyers. These attorneys have a pulse on all the interesting inventions being created within your organization—and in the broader industry.) The lawyer pointed me to a brilliant mathematician at Microsoft Cambridge, one of the company's research labs. Christian just so happened to be visiting the company headquarters, and I was able to snag an hour of his time. During our interview, he showed me a photo of the whiteboard scrawled with his now-patented algorithm. That mathematical formula vastly improved the online gaming experience. And that photograph became an integral part of Robbie's visual story to communicate the passion poured into our products.

Case Study: Message Control

An excerpt from the speech, weaving in the researcher's story:

"Think of today's Open House as the special Director's Cut where I'll share the insider stories of how my team invented—truly invented—for you. And for all of the people in your life … And for all the people you write for, whether you're *Teen Vogue* or *Newsweek* or *Engadget.*

I'm going to share what happens in our research labs in Cambridge, Israel, China, Silicon Valley. What happens at three in the morning after four weeks or four years of intensive, exhaustive teamwork. What happens after literally MILLIONS of inventor-hours ... so that all of us can experience life the way we want on the screens we care most about.

We are absolutely committed to making our Xbox LIVE experience one that's great for everyone in your family—so that you're always playing with someone who's at your level.

One of our researchers, Christian, literally played HALO for three consecutive days ... and wanted good game play. So he created this very algorithm—the matchmaker algorithm—to match all players correctly with people at their skill level on Xbox Live.

(Note: onscreen, we displayed the photograph of the whiteboard with the algorithm.)

So this researcher and his team crunched the data from 425 million games to make absolutely sure this experience works beautifully—which is surely one of the reasons why Xbox LIVE is so mainstream.

Why there are 200,000 players who participate in 1 vs. 100 every single weekend.

Why 25 million people are on Xbox LIVE, period, which is three times the number of people who watch Oprah. This is a service no other company can deliver. And it's all powered by serious technology—concepted and created and tested and retested—to make LIVE gaming for everyone serious fun.

This is one of the reasons why I can say we have the BEST and BROADEST holiday lineup in our company history. And that's really what TODAY and all of our products are all about: Welcoming you to the life you've always wanted to experience. Whenever you want. Wherever you want. However you want."

The Results

Now, consider the press coverage after this Open House event. The press quoted the speech verbatim.

"... impressive news that 425 million games had been crunched for matchmaking ... We're a bit worried about some of you ..."

— *Joystiq*

"Xbox LIVE is bigger than Oprah!"

— *Top Tweets*

"Best and broadest lineup we've ever had."

The Wall Street Journal

While good storytelling may amplify your message, pitch-perfect storytelling gives you complete word-for-word control over your message.

THREE: Story is how people understand and remember information.

Neuroscience research is clear about how people retain information. You want people to remember what you've said. This is, after all, the baseline objective of any executive communications.

Top 5 Brain Facts for Leaders

Here's a topline summary of neuroscience research with implications for leadership communications.

1. Our brains are wired to process information in narrative form. In other words, as a story.

2. Stories are how people remember information, transferring what they've learned from short-term to long-term memory.

3. People lose attention every ten minutes, and the way to recapture their attention is to hook them with a story that generates emotion.

4. Stories that evoke the biggest emotions—love, fear, sorrow, inspiration—are the most memorable.

5. People understand complex information in the shortest form of story—metaphor.[2]

FOUR: Story is how the best leaders demonstrate their authenticity.

Take a look at the research on extraordinary leaders—not merely efficient managers or good leaders. But men and women who are truly exceptional at leading. They are authentic, approachable, human. In fact, in the study *Why Should Anyone Be Led By You,* the researchers discovered, "The first quality of exceptional leaders is that they selectively reveal their weaknesses (weaknesses, not fatal flaws). Doing so lets employees see that they are approachable. It builds an atmosphere of trust and helps galvanize commitment."

So how do you be authentic? You show your humanity as a leader through the deliberate sharing of story. Your story. Your personal narrative will connect you to your employees and stakeholders.

Think about it in terms of a first date. Do you believe the person sitting across

[2] Here's a refresher course on literary devices: Metaphors are symbols that are used to describe things. For instance, when NASA discovered a truly habitable exoplanet, it explained that the planet lived in the Goldilocks zone. Specifically, "where it is neither too hot nor too cold but just right for liquid water to exist … and that is the key ingredient for … life." (See Part 3: Storycraft for more details on metaphors.)

the table from you who declares, "You know, I have a lot of personal fortitude." No, you don't. In fact, you'd probably think to yourself, "You know, you have a lot of self-esteem." What you need to hear is a story—a real example, humbly told—that showcases that internal strength. One where you draw the conclusion that your date has resilience, a characteristic that you might find worthy of a second date.

As a leader, you want to strategically share stories that demonstrate your unique strengths—and reveal a weakness.

FIVE: Stories transform customer loyalty into customer love.

In this age of ever-increasing competition for consumer attention and spending, we need our customers to move from being brand loyal to being in love with our brand. We can do that with story.

Consider this from the Mayo Clinic: "As an eight-year-old girl from Michigan was headed into surgery for a heart transplant, she asked Mike Ackerman—a pediatric cardiology fellow at Mayo who was part of her care team—if she was going to live. Dr. Ackerman said, 'Of course you're going to live, and I'm going to dance with you at your prom.' Ten years later, Dr. Ackerman flew to Michigan to surprise Stefani … at her senior prom to fulfill a promise made years ago."

Through this (short) story, here's what we glean about the Mayo Clinic: the doctors care deeply about their patients—you are in good hands. The doctors follow through—you can trust them. This is the kind of story that moves people from merely being patients or donors of the Mayo Clinic to being superfans of the Mayo Clinic.

The Short Story About Story

- Stories win people's hearts.
- Stories are the ultimate message control.
- Stories ensure people remember your message.
- Stories make you as a leader authentic, credible, and believable.
- Need proof? Check out neuroscience and leadership research.

"It is important that a leader be a good storyteller, but equally important that the leader embody that story."

—*Dr. Howard Gardner, Harvard Business School*

PART TWO:

The Leader's Stories

Heritage & Quest
Defining Moment
One Big Idea
(aka Thought Leadership)

The Trinity of Leader Stories

That cheering you hear? It's a legion of executive communications managers around the globe who are thrilled that you, as a leader, are ready to tell a story, whether in a meeting or onstage.

So let's begin by tossing out what you learned about Story in middle school.

From a leadership perspective, your stories are more than rising and falling action. Your stories are more than beginning, middle, and end. And your stories are much, much more than strict retellings of events.

The Stories You Tell as a Leader Are To:

- Transmit both your own and your organization's values and culture
- Unify your team
- Humanize yourself
- Connect your employees, customers, and constituents to a mission greater than yourselves
- Shape the way you, your team, and the industry view the world
- Mobilize change

As a leader, the top three story genres that you must craft, master, tell, and retell are:

- **Heritage & Quest:** Your organization's original and current quest story

- **Defining Moment:** Your personal narrative

- **One Big Idea:** Your thought leadership

Heritage & Quest

What Is A Heritage Story?

Storytelling is one of the most ancient of arts. Since the beginning of time, we have huddled around the campfire, sharing stories. In fact, Joseph Campbell in *The Power of Myth* posits that stories are our very culture, handed down from generation to generation to explain eternal truths. To teach the young. To provide a way to cope through different life stages. This is who we are. This is what we do when we fail. This is how we rise up. This is how we survive and thrive.

Similarly, your organization's heritage story is just as powerful, just as potent. This is especially true as a small startup because every action, every decision, every intention is shaping your heritage story.

Heritage is your organization's DNA, told through story: This is what we have always stood for.

Heritage is your organization's origin story: This is how and why we got started.

Heritage expresses your organization's eternal quest: Our North Star has always been and will always be our customer.

Without this grounding in heritage—our original quest tale—our stories are like pop-up stores, here today, gone tomorrow. They are episodic and point-in-time. They don't roll up into the greater meaning found in your organization's origin. Its genesis. Its first quest and reason for being.

For some fortunate organizations, their heritage stories are the stuff of legends.

Take **Care International.** Talk about a storied beginning. From their website: "At the beginning, there was a package: a CARE package, aimed to reduce hunger and show solidarity with the people of war-torn Europe. Seventy years ago, at the end of World War II in 1945, twenty-two American charities, a mixture of civic, religious, cooperative, and labor organizations, got together to found CARE. Originally known as the Cooperative for American Remittances to Europe, we began to deliver millions of CARE packages across Europe." And the CARE package—as well as a humanitarian organization—was born.

Or **Burton Snowboards.** Here's how the company talks about its origin. "Snowboarding invented by Jake Burton ... ah, just kidding. Jake didn't invent it, he just started the company in '77 and produced the Backhill—a narrow board with single-strap bindings and a rope and handle attached to the nose … Life on shred begins."

Or **Levi's.** "May 20, 1873 marked an historic day: the birth of the blue jean. It was on that day that Levi Strauss and Jacob Davis obtained a U.S. patent on the process of putting rivets in men's work pants for the very first time."

Inconsistent lore around your heritage saps the power of an entire organization echoing the same story. That is why you as a leader must write down the story, clarify the lore, and codify the mission, the hardships, the learnings, the eventual triumphs.

Unlike the news cycle where you tell a point-in-time story once, the heritage story gains power in the telling and retelling. That is, after all, how stories become legends. This isn't about giving an hour-long sermon reviewing the genesis of your organization every time you take the stage or meet the press, but adding a grace note reminder of why your organization started. That delicate-yet-deliberate reference to heritage—think less than a minute—in your most critical meetings and speeches is important for you as a leader.

First, you share heritage because shared history unites people into a community and gives that community an identity. Just listen to Blake Mycoskie of TOMS Shoes or Sara Blakely of Spanx wax passionate about their companies' origin stories—the aha moment and the impetus behind their brands.

Second, you share heritage because you sound presidential. Your history gives you the halo effect of gravitas. Scour any presidential State of the Union address, and you'll hear references like this: "For 200 years, we've put our shoulders against the wheel of progress." In twelve short words, you can hear how elegantly and neatly that heritage illuminates some of America's core values: Ingenuity. Work ethic. Resilience.

Third, you share heritage as a guiding light, especially when you are in the midst of change management or a large strategic shift. Think about Alan Mulally, who dug into the company archives in the first couple of weeks after starting as CEO of Ford. He knew he needed to uncover his new company's heritage—its soul. He found that heritage in one of the first ads Ford ran in 1925, promising that Ford was "Opening the highways for all mankind." Before the Model-T, driving was an elitist pursuit; Ford democratized driving. Mulally hung that ad on his office wall. Then he distributed that ad to his leaders: This is who we were and why we existed. And who we still are. This is our North Star. This is our heritage.

Crafting Your Heritage Story

Finding, developing, and sharing your corporate heritage story is some of the most important work that YOU as Chief Inspiration Officer can do. It is pride. It is culture. It is values.

Let's (re)create your corporate heritage story.

STEP ONE. Find your corporate heritage story.

Scour your website for your heritage story. And if it's not there, check out the last couple of annual reports. If you lead a large organization and have the luxury of archives, make a field trip. Otherwise, you may have to start from scratch (skip to Step Three).

STEP TWO. Analyze your heritage story.

- Does the story articulate the major facts—who, what, where, why, when, and how?

- Do you get a sense of your company's personality through the voice?

- Do your company's values shine through?

- Is there a good balance between humility and pride?

- Are there telling details that make you feel as if you were there right at the start?

_____

_____

_____

_____

_____

_____

_____

_____

_____

_____

_____

_____

_____

_____

_____

STEP THREE. Investigate your heritage story.

If any of the answers in Step Two are a no, then you have the fun of hunting down the delicious details that will enliven the story with personality.

Interview three movers and shakers from the early days, if possible. Ask them what it was like to work at the organization back then. Listen for interesting turns of phrases that capture the energy and vibe of that time. If your company is, say, a hundred years old, then read as many primary source documents as you can find—whether those were old articles, marketing materials, or letters.

Questions like these are the most effective in drawing out stories and sound bites:

- Give me seven words that describe our company when it started.

- What were your most memorable moments in the first two years?

- What makes you laugh or smile when you think about the early days?

- What do you miss about the early days? What don't you miss?

_____

_____

_____

_____

_____

_____

_____

_____

_____

_____

_____

STEP FOUR. Find a magical object that represents your heritage.

The best heritage stories are anchored with an actual object from the founding days. These artifacts carry history and emotion.

For instance, consider Levi's heritage story from their website: "May 20, 1873 marked an historic day: the birth of the blue jean. It was on that day that Levi Strauss and Jacob Davis obtained a U.S. patent on the process of putting rivets in men's work pants for the very first time."

If you want an artifact that powerfully represents Levi's heritage, it's the rivet. That simple metal rivet represents everything about Levi's: its bold innovation. Its commitment to quality. Its deep understanding and passion for customers. That rivet is one powerful magical object.

Now, ask yourself:

• What is your organization's magical object?

• What does it represent?

STEP FIVE. Add depth and personality to your heritage story.

You have the facts of your organization's beginning—probably codified somewhere on the website. That is the who, what, where, why, and when. Now it's time to add voice, compelling details, and mission.

Review your interview notes. Are there two or three phrases that jump out at you, that make you say, "Yes! That is exactly what those early days must have been like!" For instance, remember Burton Snowboards—"Life on shred begins." That one phrase authentically captures snowboard culture. Inside secret of the best leaders: Name and claim a catchphrase that's repeatable and fresh. That's how you grab the attention of your board, your peers, and your team. With the right tweetable phrase, you can break through to customers and donors. You can even penetrate pop culture.

Are there two or three phrases that illuminate your organization's culture and values? For instance, "Like most startups, Microsoft is flexible hours and no dress code, team pride and witty code names. A company that eats its own dog food."

Is your organization mission embedded in the heritage story? With the Microsoft example, the mission is: "A computer on every desktop and in every home."

Can you foreshadow your future success? With Burton Snowboards: "Snowboarding invented by Jake Burton … ah, just kidding. Jake didn't invent it, he just started the company in '77 … " While Jake may not have created snowboarding, he did invent the snowboard industry.

_____

_____

STEP SIX. Share your heritage story.

If you want to sound presidential, you need to weave your heritage story into your major keynotes, whether with internal or external audiences. Again, we're not talking about a huge, big, long history lecture. Think less than a minute. Think a light touch.

For instance, recall the rivet, the magical object for Levi's. If I were coaching Levi's leaders, I'd say, "Always, always, always carry a rivet with you, tucked into your jeans, whenever you meet the press, conduct an important meeting, or get onstage." And during the emotional high point of the meeting or speech, you take out that rivet. You hold it in your cupped hand. You slowly unfurl your fingers. You share that rivet. Because. That rivet communicates the heart and soul of Levi's.

And perhaps the words—depending on the intention of the speech—is something as short as this: "We at Levi's have always been RIVETED on our customers." Behind the leader on an enormous screen is a close up of one single rivet and only that rivet. There you go, heritage expressed. By invoking heritage, we have also communicated our longstanding North Star (customer, customer, customer). And culture (we are and have always been customer obsessed and innovation focused). And values (we are all about enduring quality and loving our customer).

_____

_____

_____

_____

_____

_____

_____

_____

_____

Homework

- What speech can you use to test your heritage story?

- Where is the emotional high point in your speech? Can you prime that moment even more with the heritage story? Or can you close out that moment with the grace note of heritage?

_____

_____

_____

_____

_____

_____

_____

_____

_____

_____

_____

_____

_____

_____

_____

_____

_____

_____

_____

A Special Note For Leaders of Startups

You may be thinking to yourself: *Well, my organization is so new, our heritage is what happened yesterday.*

Actually, your heritage is happening right now. Your heritage is the reason you conceived your organization in the first place. What idea arrested your imagination and captured your every waking moment? What problem couldn't you shake? Why are you throwing yourself—heart, body, soul—into this endeavor? Why are you sacrificing time and treasure to create this organization for your future customers?

Whatever the answers, those are the inception point of your heritage. Boil your answers down to a few pithy sentences and share the WHY whenever you talk about your organization.

Study how Blake Mycoskie of TOMS concisely and poignantly tells his organization's origin story. There he was on vacation in Argentina when he noticed all the barefooted kids. He quickly learned that the mere wearing of shoes could prevent diseases and get children to school. A company was born from his sailboat of a home, a $5,000 investment, and a commitment to give a pair of shoes away for every pair bought. There's the heritage of a startup, rolled up into a quest.

Coaching to Make Your Heritage Story Pop

Most of us can recite the story of our organization's beginnings. But to make the heritage story resonate in the heart and mind, you'll want to look for the juicy details. Luscious details that make people feel as if they were there at the ground level. Details that give the story a sense of time and place. Details that communicate the vibe of the time and the urgency of the founders.

Let's take a closer look at how Burton Snowboards was able to communicate all that in three economical sentences.

Burton Snowboards' heritage story from the company website:

"Snowboarding invented by Jake Burton ... ah, just kidding. Jake didn't invent it, he just started the company in '77 and produced the Backhill—a narrow board with single strap bindings and a rope and handle attached to the nose ... Life on shred begins."

Note the voice
- "ah, just kidding." And again "life on shred begins." That captures the company's irreverence, then and now.

Note the humility
- "Jake didn't invent it..."

Yet note the pride
- "... he just started the company..."

Note the sense of time
- "in '77"

Note the detail to anchor the story in the company's first snowboard
- "the Backhill." Named and claimed.

Note the specific sensory details so we can envision the first snowboard
- "a *narrow* board with *single strap* bindings and a *rope* and *handle* attached to the *nose.*"

Now, let's look at Microsoft's heritage story from its website:

"It's the 1970s. At work, we rely on typewriters. If we need to copy a document, we likely use a mimeograph or carbon paper. Few have heard of microcomputers, but two young computer enthusiasts, Bill Gates and Paul Allen, see that personal computing is a path to the future. In 1975, Gates and Allen form a partnership called Microsoft. Like most startups, Microsoft begins small, but has a huge vision—a computer on every desktop and in every home. During the next years, Microsoft begins to change the ways we work."

The facts are clear: 1975, Gates and Allen, Microsoft vision. But how can we insert more voice so we get a real sense of the company? How can we feel its startup energy? How do we know what it valued then and now?

We listen to what some of the first employees say about working, living, breathing Microsoft in the early days. Read a few quotes from some interviews I conducted with superstars from back in the day.

QUESTION
Can you describe Microsoft in the early days?

ANSWER
We were IQ over experience.

ANSWER
Work hard, play hard. Getting stuff done.

ANSWER
Flexible hours & no dress code.

ANSWER
Team pride and witty code names.

ANSWER

Unapologetically competitive AND intensely self-critical. A belief in personal empowerment and long-term time horizon.

ANSWER

We are the company that has eaten our own dog food. In the shrimp vs. weenie wars, we devoured weenies.

ANSWER

Speaking the truth even if BillG was rocking back and forth really fast.

ANSWER

Being committed, wanting to win, taking and giving criticism. It wasn't at all formal and generally was a meritocracy. You got ahead faster by being good than by being popular. Risk-taking was admired and rewarded. It was definitely geeky. You did not get points for driving a Beemer, but coding in Assembler? Making ginger ale come out of your nose? Alpha.

Talk about storytelling gold! From these details, you get a sense of energy, passion, commitment from eight interviews with company old-timers and superstars. (Note: this took all of three hours to conduct and collect over Facebook messaging.)

So let's freshen up Microsoft's heritage story with the voice of the coders and their unbridled energy while condensing for pacing. At the same time, we can foreshadow the current corporate messaging.

"It's the 1970s. Bellbottoms. Typewriters. Carbon paper. But few microcomputers ... until two young geeks, Bill Gates and Paul Allen, bet that personal computing could change the way the world works. In 1975, they form Microsoft. Like most startups, Microsoft is flexible hours and no dress code, team pride, and witty code names. A company that eats its own dog food. A company that starts small and envisions huge—a computer on every desktop and in every home. Alpha."

Note the voice
- "no dress code, team pride, and witty code names." And again ending it with the geeky affirmation: "Alpha." That captures the company's energy, then and now.

Note the humility
- "*two young geeks,* Bill Gates and Paul Allen bet that personal computing..." These geeks bet—they made a calculated gamble. Success was anything but a sure thing.

Yet note the boldness
- "...change the way the world works..."

Note the sense of time and how economically we can communicate that with a few details
- "It's the 1970s. Bellbottoms. Typewriters. Carbon paper." Delete the extraneous words from the original heritage story and you speed the pace, which communicates the urgency of that time. As well, it serves to get us to the heart of the story faster: the two young geeks and their unapologetically ambitious quest.

Note the detail to anchor the story in its long held values
- "A company that ate its own dog food." In other words, we relentlessly work the tech to protect our customers.

Note the foreshadowing of its future success
- "A company that *starts* small..." Fast forward to Windows 95 with its iconic Start button.

And importantly, note the details that get left out. Though wonderful—"unapologetically competitive and intensely self-critical"—those descriptions may not necessarily be consistent with the company's more collaborative culture today. Some great information will be left on the cutting room floor.

"Say it, reader. Say the word 'quest' out loud. It is an extraordinary word, isn't it? So small and yet so full of wonder, so full of hope."

—Kate DiCamillo, *The Tale of Despereaux*

The Quest

What Is a Quest?

As a leader, you must be able to articulate your organization's Purpose, its reason for being. This clarity helps you and your team to stay focused even in the midst of turmoil and change. Even better, recast your organizational Purpose into a Quest—a story about your team of heroes who want to accomplish some big, audacious goal—and you'll harness every bit of power that is storytelling. You'll tap into the age-old well of passion and tension, energy and emotion, trials and triumphs. No longer stuck with dry pabulum, you'll wield a memorable, rousing narrative filled with adventures, some mishaps, and persevering heroes. And importantly, through this particular story, you will invite every single member of your team, every one of your constituents, to be part of your Quest.

Joseph Campbell, the mythologist, wrote in his book *Hero of A Thousand Faces* that our most epic tales are quests—stories about heroes who desperately want something and must overcome obstacles in order to attain what they want. So talk about your Purpose in the form of a Quest, and capture people's imaginations about a cause that they feel passionate about at a soul-deep level. Woo them to be part of your team of heroes. And anoint them to embark on the quest with you.

What is your organization's *Lord of the Rings* quest? What is your purpose of epic Harry Potter proportions?

Ask yourself:

- What does your organization want desperately?
- What obstacles has it overcome already?
- What obstacles must it still overcome?

Amplifing Quest With Heritage

If you want to turbocharge the importance of your quest, then you as a leader need to deploy your heritage strategically and skillfully. When you weave your heritage into your quest, you insert a sense of veritas and gravitas: *We have already succeeded (or learned greatly) in our original quest, and this next quest is even more important.* You communicate your longstanding commitment to the cause that may have predated even you yourself: *We have always had this North Star.* Using your heritage, you create an aura of *fait accompli*, the belief that there is no other option but your organization's ultimate success: *We were successful in changing the world the first time. So you can bet that we will change the world again.*

As a side note: for those leading startups, grounding your communications with your quest and heritage is especially important. Put in another—albeit zen koan-Yoda—way your very heritage is your quest. Every word, every decision, every action can potentially be immortalized into your quest tale. So make sure that you are leading in a way that is worthy of an epic tale.

Case Studies

ONE

Levi's weaves heritage with quest brilliantly in their website: "Anyone can make a pair of blue jeans, but Levi Strauss & Co. made the first blue jean—in 1873. And we draw upon our heritage to continually reinvent the blue jean for generation after generation."

Note the heritage
- We made the first blue jean—in 1873.

Note the subtle nod to the original quest
- We invented the blue jeans, durable pants for miners.

Note the new quest
- To continually *reinvent* the blue jean for generation after generation.

TWO

Here's an excerpt from a speech for a Gates Foundation leader, showing how an organization's heritage and mission were used to extend into a bold new quest:

"We are so lucky that Bill and Melinda (Gates) are great advocates for the issues they care about. Because of who they are and what they stand for and how they work, our Gates Foundation brand is pretty well known. My hope is that we deploy our brand to help our partners to achieve their goals."

Note the implied heroes
- Bill, Melinda, and the rest of us at the Gates Foundation.

Note all the obstacles that have been overcome, a message embedded in the unstated litany of accomplishments
- We have been great advocates for hard, seemingly intractable issues.

Note as well that this litany serves a second purpose, which is to create the sense of *fait accompli*
- If we were able to do all of this—against all odds and some global skepticism—then surely we will be able to execute on our next quest.

Note the nod to heritage
- Bill and Melinda, who they are, and what they stand for.

Note the new quest is even more audacious than the original quest
- Deploy that brand so that there is a halo effect to help our partners.

Defining Moment

What Is a Defining Moment?

In novels and screenplays, there is a general tenet that the main character needs to do something or say something that demonstrates that this is a hero worth watching for ninety minutes or cheering on over the duration of 400 pages. The late screenwriter and producer Blake Synder called this the "Save the Cat" moment.

In *Skyfall,* for instance, the Bond film begins with 007 leaping over the cloistered rooftops of Istanbul. He barges into a dark room. There, bleeding out, is his fellow spy. Bond drops to his knees, presses his hand to the wound, and is going to stay … until M orders him to forge on. We like Bond at that moment because we see that deep down he's got a heart. He's honorable. He is worthy of our emotional investment. He saved the cat!

Similarly, as a leader, the most powerful and immediate way you can create connection, build trust, and enhance your credibility is through sharing your personal story.

Not just any story, but a story that shows how you have handled trials and hardship and challenges in your past. A story that showcases how much you've learned and grown as a person. A story that illuminates your values and principles. A story where you quite possibly Save the Cat. From a speechwriter's perspective, you must Save the Cat within the first five to eight minutes of being onstage.

Why Save the Cat as a leader?

Consider the research on extraordinary leaders. Studies have shown that truly exceptional leaders have been tested and transformed personally, often by traumatic crises.

Consider that these same extraordinary leaders know who they are at the core because they have survived unexpected, difficult experiences.

In fact, Warren Bennis, the pioneer of Leadership Studies, found, "One of the most reliable indicators and predictors of true leadership is an individual's ability to find meaning in negative events and to learn from even the most trying circumstances."

Put another way: One of the very strongest metals on earth is tamahagane, also known as Jewel Steel. It is an art to create this steel from iron sand and charcoal. A team of four or five craftsmen smelt and forge and fold and refold the compound up to thirty-five times. It's that very process of melting at intense heat and the painstaking folding and refolding that makes Jewel Steel so uniquely strong ... and beautiful.

Every. Single. Successful leader I have ever worked with or coached has more than GRIT. They have tamahagane grit. They are men and women who've gotten stronger, not because they have a long track record of success. But because they've been smelted and forged by crushing obstacles.

They. Are. Tamahagane. Leaders.

Over and over again, in their personal stories, they show courage, mental toughness, and maturity to learn from their traumas and failures.

Tamahagane Leaders demonstrate passion, willpower, and personal persistence to achieve their goals no matter the obstacle or setback or failure.

Tamahagane Leaders display the commitment to stretch themselves and stick to difficult conditions even—and especially—when things aren't going well.

Tamahagane Leaders have led their teams and divisions and countries and companies through trials by fire—economic downturns, political turmoil, and devastating natural disasters. Not all of them have suffered dire tragedies—defied death, been orphaned at a young age, survived alcoholic parents—although some have … and are stronger for it. But they have all been everyday heroes who quite possibly commit the most courageous act onstage: they can laugh at their own foibles. They can share their own stories of professional despair. They can get real and vulnerable. And in so doing, they credibly share hard-won wisdom that comes only from failure. Insight that materializes only through hindsight.

They are leaders you can trust now and in the future. Because. Not everything is going to go the way their beautifully architected strategies have planned. Here's the truth: We will ALL fall down. And we will ALL need to spring back up. What counts is how we spring back up after we fall. And these are leaders who have sprung back up before even harder, more crushing circumstances.

As an audience, we trust these Tamahagane Leaders—especially if we know their story. And that means that we have to *hear* their story.

In politics, a platform is a candidate's succinctly stated values and actions, pulled together to garner support for different topics and issues. Similarly, the first thing you must do as a leader is to build out your own presidential platform: This is who I am. This is what I stand for. This is my purpose. These are the principles that govern my life and decision-making. And here are my unique strengths as a leader. In other words, here is why you can trust me.

The basis of these presidential platforms? Your own personal narratives. Your "hero" story. Please note that this isn't an I-am-so-great ode to narcissism story. This is the here's-how-I-survived story.

Only after I uncover a leader's "hero" story do I tackle the typical questions communications experts will ask leaders. So after you create your narrative, then— and only then—answer these questions.

- What's the legacy you want to leave?

  _____

  _____

- How are you leaving the organization stronger than when you first started?

  _____

  _____

- Who has had the greatest impact on you? Why?

  _____

  _____

- What are your most important values?

  _____

  _____

- What motivates you?

  _____

  _____

- What are your favorite novels, favorite movies, favorite sports—and what have you learned from them?

  _____

  _____

- What's on your worry list?

  _____

  _____

Note: Make sure you fill in the blanks on the previous page. All of my executives have used answers to these very questions in breakthrough speeches that humanize them and define their leadership. But the two most important questions that I think audiences want to know as soon as an executive takes the stage:

Who are you ... really?

_____

_____

_____

_____

And why should I believe you?

_____

_____

_____

_____

"Where there is ruin, there is hope for a treasure."

—*Rumi*

Why You Must Share Your Story

If you're hyperventilating—or feeling any resistance at all—about sharing your story, take a deep breath and consider this: All of my executives have experienced professional breakthrough moments onstage because they shared their personal breakthrough story.

Career-changing and career-making breakthrough moments: "Clear. Focused. Passionate. Believable."

Perception-shifting moments: "This is the first time I believed in him."

Leadership-defining moments: Their approval ratings skyrocketed post-speech ... because they established their credibility through sharing their story.

Each of these leaders strategically shared elements of their personal story. Specifically, their I-have-grit story. Their I-am-the-right-leader-now story.

By showing a soupçon of vulnerability onstage, these leaders strengthened their leadership. They became approachable and believable—because they endured hardship. They demonstrated their personal strengths, or superpowers—because they prevailed. They got real onstage—because they showed humility. As a result, they connected with their audiences in a deep, profound, self-revelatory way.

Just take a look at Steve Jobs' commencement speech at Stanford, given in 2005 with 33.5 million views on YouTube. People still talk about that speech today because of the insight and wisdom gleaned from his personal stories.

Jobs revealed, "My biological mother was a young, unwed college graduate student, and she decided to put me up for adoption." That statement alone is pretty self-revelatory. But he continued, "She felt very strongly that I should be adopted by college graduates, so everything was all set for me to be adopted at birth by a lawyer and his wife. Except that when I popped out they decided at the last minute that they really wanted a girl. So my parents, who were on a waiting list, got a call in the middle of the night asking: 'We have an unexpected baby boy; do you want him?' They said: 'Of course.' My biological mother later found out that my mother had never graduated from college and that my father had never graduated from high school. She refused to sign the final adoption papers. She only relented a few months later when my parents promised that I would someday go to college."

Importantly, Jobs used his personal story to teach a point about how life is all interconnected. But more than that, we connect with him as a person. We know how serendipitous life can be because we have all experienced that—just as we have experienced the need to belong, the need to count, the need to be wanted.

Those driving needs are shared across all humanity. That's why when you share your vulnerability—what you wanted more than anything, the obstacles you had to muster every bit of your grit to overcome—you build a bridge directly to your audience.

In other words, through your story, you reveal the universal in the specific. Once you do that, as a novelist, your reader doesn't just care about your character, but connects deeply with your character. The same is true with a leader and the audience.

Share your story and your listener doesn't just care, but connects. Story is the bridge to trust and belief.

Three Important Notes About Sharing Your Story

The leaders who share their personal stories aren't randomly opening their pasts for people's inspection and critique. This is not a therapy session for public consumption. This is not emotional manipulation of your audience so they will like you. Instead, these leaders are strategically giving people an important insight into who they are at their very core.

FIRST, the stories extraordinary leaders share have business relevance. These are stories that instill confidence in their audiences that they are the exact right leader for the particular business challenge their organizations or teams are facing.

SECOND, extraordinary leaders are judicious with detail. These aren't lengthy, disastrous first-date, let-me-tell-you-my-life-story monologues. Instead, they share just enough of their story—none more than two minutes long—to communicate their inner steeliness in the face of difficulty and for the audience to appreciate what they endured.

THIRD, extraordinary leaders understand that the personal stories they share are supposed to be instructional and inspirational. In fact, your moment of truth story doesn't have to be doom-and-gloom: My mom died and my dad abandoned us! The one element that the story you share must have is how you personally overcame obstacles. That is how story straddles being instructive: this is how we prevail. And inspiration: If I have prevailed in the past, we will prevail now.

Case Studies

ONE

Immediately when I started working for Robbie Bach, then the President of Microsoft Entertainment & Devices, we knew that he had to give one of his most challenging speeches before 14,000 global salespeople at the Philips Arena in Atlanta. So I brought him onstage where he immediately shared his defining moment, a story that he recounts in his book, *Xbox Revisited: A Game Plan for Corporate and Civic Renewal.*

Here's what Robbie revealed about his personal backstory to the entire sales force: "A lot of you don't know me personally. So let me tell you a little story. I've been a tennis player my whole life. But when I was thirteen, I grew eight inches, sprouting over half an inch every single month for a year. I was bent over at a forty-degree angle. So starting in middle school, arguably hell housed on earth, I had to wear a metal ring around my neck that was connected to a girdle around my waist, all tethered together with metal rods to keep my back straight. On top of that, my family moved from Wisconsin to North Carolina. Doctor's orders were to wear the brace virtually 24/7."

Now on top of that diagnosis, the doctors told Robbie that he was no longer able to play football and basketball. Robbie continued in his speech: "BUT. There was no way I was going to let an exoskeleton slow me down, and even if I had to give up what I really loved—basketball—I was still going to play a sport. So even covered in metal, I still played tennis. I still won my matches. I still became a nationally ranked player."

Robbie stared out at the rapt audience that filled the sporting arena and promised, "Guess what? We are all still playing tennis."

That story, simply told, won Robbie his first standing ovation and his highest speaking scores of his career.

TWO

Another one of my executives, Sue Bevington, Corporate Vice President of HR at Microsoft, changed the way the top 1,000 senior executives at her company viewed her by sharing her Moment of Truth story.

On her vacations, Sue builds houses through Habitat for Humanity. On one trip, she was asked to remodel an older home in Los Angeles. It was three and a half stories tall perched on a steep hill. The ladder to scrape and paint the top floor was leaning at such a terrifying angle, it looked as if one small breeze would topple it over. Not one person on her team volunteered. So Sue climbed up there herself, sweaty palms and all, for the entire week. A job had to be done.

Sue followed that story with this call to action: "We're facing our biggest—and arguably, most important Moment of Truth with 10 major launches against some of our toughest competitors. And it's going to be hard work to win. But. A job must be done."

Note: Sue also got the highest speaker scores of her career with this speech.

THREE

And if you want to see vulnerable, watch Amy Cuddy's TED talk, titled, "Your body language shapes who you are."

At 16:00, listen carefully, which is easy to do since Amy grabs your attention by revealing, "When I was nineteen, I was in a really bad car accident … I was thrown from the car. And I woke up in a head-injury rehab ward, and I had been withdrawn from college, and I learned that my I.Q. had dropped by two standard deviations, which was very traumatic. I knew my I.Q. because I had identified with being smart, and I had been called gifted as a child."

Note: That TED talk has garnered 6.7 million views since she gave it two years ago.

Superpowers

From this see-my-grit story, the audience is able to glean a leader's core strengths.

Through Robbie Bach's story about his brace, we know he's persistent. Risk-taking. Competitive. Gritty. A survivor. Those are his superpowers.

From Sue Bevington whose vacations are spent on Habitat for Humanity missions, we know she's gutsy. Team-oriented. Mission-focused. Big-hearted. And yes, oh so very gritty. Those are her superpowers.

From Amy Cuddy, we have a pretty good sense that she's crazy intelligent, courageous, and compassionate. And gritty. You better believe she has grit. Those are her superpowers.

What are your superpowers?

And what are the stories that best illuminate your superpowers?

Coaching For The Story Reluctant

If you're still skeptical about sharing your story, then witness the power of sharing someone else's I-have-tamahagane-grit story instead to illustrate your values and principles.

When one VP wanted to communicate the importance of humility in leadership, she shared this story about a peer who told her: "I don't view my role as the largest player. I go back to my humble beginnings where my family was sharecroppers. When I travel, I tell my folks, 'Don't stand on ceremony too much.' When you show up as an exec, they pull out all the stops: the car waiting at the airport. As long as I have an address, I'll take a cab."

(Note: one of the most powerful ways to build bridges across an organization is to share your peers' stories. As a basic executive-communications rule, I encourage my leaders to include at least two stories about peers or team members in a twenty-minute speech, three in a forty-five-minute keynote.)

And if sharing a peer's story still seems daunting, then share a story about one of your heroes. When one executive wanted to show other leaders in a keynote how to dilemma flip—see hope where others see hopelessness—she used the tamahagane-grit story of Seahawks quarterback, Russell Wilson.

"Let's take a look at Russell Wilson, quarterback of the Seahawks. Critics said he was too short to be a quarterback. Critics said that the Seahawks coach made a disastrous mistake by picking Russell in the third round of the draft. Well. Repeat after me: Super Bowl Champ!

"Russell talks about how his father died four years ago, and how his father used to wake him up at 5:30 every morning to teach him about work ethic and how his father would ask him, 'Why not you, Russell? Why not you?' So at the beginning of the 2014 season, Russell said to his team, 'Hey, why not us?'"

Harvest stories from your leadership team, your partners, your employees, your customers, and your favorite heroes. Is there a tamahagane grit story that you can share that underscores a point that you want to make?

Quick Assessment

- What personal stories can you share to connect with your employees, customers, press, stakeholders—and convince them that you are the right leader? That they can trust you as a person? That they can believe in you as their leader, particularly if you are leading them into uncharted territory—a new strategy, a new product direction, a new industry to pursue?

- Since the best leaders have grit, have you shared a story that proves your grit?

Finding Your Story

The single most powerful story you can—and must—share onstage as a leader is your Defining Moment Story. Your own personal Save the Cat decision. This is the moment that demarcated a clear before and after in your life. One that tested you to your very core. One that delivered a hard blow, but not a death blow because you persevered. You prevailed. You called on every bit of your inner strength. And you didn't just survive the test, but the test strengthened you. It's in this crucible moment where the skills and strengths that powered your survival have come to define you as a leader.

Let's find your story.

STEP ONE: Work with a trusted confidante.

Hopefully, this is your chief storyteller, your director of executive communications. (Note: if you aren't calling in that person, then ask yourself if you're working with the right storyteller.) And if you don't have a chief storyteller (yet), then invite someone you trust implicitly to hear the good, bad, and ugly of your life story.

STEP TWO: Get into storytelling mode.

We want you to be in your most natural storytelling state just as if you were catching up with your best friend.

First, tell us about how you refuel. Do you refurbish vintage Mini Coopers? Hit golf balls? Escape to an island? Trek in a new locale? Go on Habitat for Humanity missions? Tell us about the best moment you've ever had refueling in this way. Or the last time you refueled.

_____

_____

_____

_____

_____

Second, tell us about your heroes, whether a president, athlete, parent, everyday person, or fictional character.

- Who are they and why are they your heroes?
- What do you admire about them?
- What have you learned from them?

_____

_____

_____

_____

_____

STEP THREE. Get real.

Tell us about the single worst moment of your life—whether personal, professional, or philanthropic.

- What did you want?
- What happened instead?
- What trials or circumstances nearly felled you to your knees?
- How did you feel?
- Then what happened?
- What did you do?
- What did you learn?
- How did it change the way you viewed yourself? The world?
- What opportunities were created for you because of this experience?
- How has this experience informed the way you lead?

_____

_____

_____

_____

_____

_____

_____

_____

_____

_____

_____

_____

_____

_____

_____

_____

_____

STEP FOUR. Identify your superpowers.

Based on that Defining Moment in your life, what are your top three superpowers, or strengths?

1. _____

2. _____

3. Tamahagane Grit.

STEP FIVE: Become the short story author of your life.

Let's pull together the key elements of your story, using the framework that mythologist Joseph Campbell has named The Hero's Journey. Think of your favorite epic stories—whether *Lord of the Rings* or Harry Potter. Generally they follow the cycle of a hero embarking on a quest, enduring a number of trials, and returning transformed.

Write one to three sentences per plot point in your own hero's journey story.

- Existing World (what was your life like before the Defining Moment?):

  _____

  _____

  _____

- Call to Adventure (what changed your world?):

  _____

  _____

  _____

- Crossing Threshold (what was your new world like?):

  _____

  _____

  _____

- Road of Trials (what obstacles or hardships did you encounter?):

  _____

  _____

  _____

- Belly of the Whale (what was the absolute worst moment in your ordeal?):

  _____

  _____

  _____

- The Reward (what did you do? What did you learn?):

  _____

  _____

  _____

As an example, let's dissect Robbie Bach's story about his back brace to pinpoint the key turning points.

Existing World: When Robbie was twelve, everything was happy in Wisconsin where he excelled at football and basketball.

Call to Adventure: When Robbie turned thirteen, he grew eight inches in a year. The problem was: his spine didn't keep up with the rest of his growth, and he was bent over at a forty-degree angle.

Crossing Threshold: Robbie found himself wearing a back brace. As Robbie writes in his book, *Xbox Revisited,* "The brace wrapped a full leather girdle around my waist, a metal bar straight in front of my chest, and two additional bars along my back. The bars attached at the top to a ring that circled my neck with a chin-rest in the front. I would slide into it from the back, tighten a screw at the back of the neck ring, and cinch up the girdle with a strap to tighten it around my waist."

Road of Trials: On top of that grim diagnosis, he had to stop playing basketball and football.

Belly of the Whale: When his family moved from Wisconsin to North Carolina that same year, Robbie felt like such a social outcast, he didn't want to leave his room.

Reward: His mom suggested that he pick up tennis. Within a year, Robbie was nationally ranked.

STEP SIX: Revision.

Rewrite your personal narrative as if it were the back-cover copy for your memoir. Can you write your story in 100 words or fewer?

_____

_____

_____

_____

_____

_____

_____

STEP SEVEN: Voice lessons.

Now read what you wrote aloud. Does it sound like you? If not, write for your ear—because you're writing this to be shared aloud. We're not talking fancy, fussy, convoluted language. So rewrite in the language that sounds like the most authentic, real you, chatting with your inner circle of trusted people.

_____

_____

_____

_____

_____

_____

_____

STEP EIGHT: Superpowers and the Extraordinary Leader.

Now review your story with a last lens, the traits of the extraordinary leader. Are you showing up with these particular attributes:

Real

Gritty

Self-aware

Humble

Growth-centered

Along with these traits, are your top three unique strengths—your superpowers—showing up in your story?

STEP NINE. Sharing your insight through an impact line.

The first sentence after sharing your story serves as so much more than a transition. It must drive to a business impact. That sentence is the entire reason why you are sharing your story.

Recall how the President of Microsoft Entertainment used his commitment to playing tennis while wearing a back brace to underscore his point that the company was still intent on winning. He said, "Guess what? *We are all still playing tennis.*"

Translation: Yes, market share for one of our products has dropped. But guess what? We are still in the game.

Or remember how the VP of HR for the same company used her story to rally leaders: "We're facing our biggest—and arguably, most important—Moment of Truth with ten major launches against some of our toughest competitors. And it's going to be hard work to win. *But. A job must be done.*"

Translation: Yes, this next six months are going to be scary hard. But a leader must lead. So go do your job and lead.

Notice how the impact line both refers back to the personal story *and* communicates the business message.

So ask yourself:

- What is your impact line going to be?
- Is it referencing back to your personal story and at the same time landing the main business message?

STEP TEN. Test-drive your story.

It's time to take your story out for a test run. So pick a smaller venue with a receptive audience to share your story onstage. Aim for ninety seconds, or a maximum of two minutes, for telling your personal story. And lastly, try to place the story within the first five to eight minutes of taking the stage.

One Last Note About Your Story

If you feel at all uncertain about the need and reason for getting vulnerable onstage, remind yourself that we all love stories of survival. We yearn for phoenix resurrections where the hero is felled and rises stronger than ever. We as a world need leaders who have been tested and retested with failures and who demonstrate their inner core of grit.

Grit is, after all, strength with spirit. Fortitude on fire. Resilience after ruin.

We seek this very quality in our leaders. So show us what you're made of. Tell us through your personal story about your grit. And when you do, you inspire us to follow your lead.

"The ancestor of every action is
a thought."

—*Ralph Waldo Emerson*

One Big Idea

(aka Thought Leadership)

What Is Thought Leadership?

Ever wondered what differentiated the TED talks that generated millions of views and catapulted some speakers into superstar status? Check out Brené Brown and her Power of Vulnerability talk, if you don't happen to be among her 21.5 million viewers. Here is a professor who researched in relative obscurity until she took the big stage to espouse an idea that completely inverted our perspective and beliefs. Her incendiary worldview: Vulnerability is the seat of strength.

The popularity of Brené's TED talk makes sense when you consider what Jeremy Donovan, one of the TEDx organizers, discerned about the most popular of the speeches. He explained, "If you had to say there was one magical element to the best TED talks, it's that those speakers picked one really, really big idea." What TED calls One Really, Really, Big Idea, authors call worldview, academics call sensemaking, and executives call thought leadership.

Whatever you name it, articulating a distinct point of view is one of the most important jobs a leader has today. In fact, Peter Drucker, the management expert, said that one of the most crucial jobs of a CEO is to go out into the world, filter it through their worldview, listen to all the weak signals, and bring back those key learnings in a distilled, understandable way.

Top 5 Questions Thought Leaders Ask

What do the market trends, the competition, the customers and their changing needs mean for us?

What are the futurists and analysts saying?

What's at stake? Why is this important now? Why should we care?

After all that research, do you see a convergence of trends?

Can you drive that convergence into an epiphany, one that is startling and fresh and carries huge implications?

Distill the convergence of trends into One Big Idea, and that is your thought leadership.

Take Kristin Rowe-Finkbeiner, CEO and co-founder of momsrising. org. She is one of the top thought leaders on motherhood issues in America. Here's a snapshot of some of her thought leadership on inequality: "Women without children make 90 cents to a man's dollar, mothers make only 73 cents, single moms make about 60 cents to a man's dollar, and women of color experience increased wage hits on top of that. Mothers with equal resumes are hired 80 percent less of the time than non-mothers and are offered lower starting salaries."

What that all means is this: "Motherhood is now a greater predictor of inequality than gender in America."

Startling, isn't it? She advances a provocative new way to look at a longstanding issue. That is Kristin's One Big Idea.

As a leader, what's your One Big Idea?

Why Thought Leadership Matters

Your One Big Idea—thought leadership—isn't specifically about your organization, your product, or your campaign. It is higher-level thinking. It is espousing a worldview of the entire industry, issue area, or planet at large. It is cartography where you are mapmaking the world of data, trends, and human needs. As a mapmaker, you are drawing the clean boundary lines in a messy, chaotic, uncharted world. And then as a leader, you are extracting the meaning for the rest of us. You are saying, "Look. Here's what I'm seeing. And here's why this matters for all of us now."

What Steve Jobs said about simplicity can be applied to thought leadership:

"Simple can be harder than complex. You have to work hard to get your thinking clean to make it simple. But it's worth it in the end because once you get there, you can move mountains."

—*Steve Jobs*

Thought leadership matters because you are providing your audience with an insight that is the very expression of simplicity: a concise articulation of what's really going on underneath the surface. And with that insight, you can win support and instigate change with your compelling strategy and plan.

Let's go back to Kristin Rowe-Finkbeiner from the earlier section. Here's a thought leader who pored over reams of economic data to drive to the surprising—and surprisingly simple—epiphany: *Motherhood* is now a greater predictor of inequality than gender in America.

As a leader, you deploy your thought leadership before you advance your vision, strategy, and plan. In fact, thought leadership informs all of those. So consider it the prelude, the opening act before your strategy. Articulated well, thought leadership makes your strategy *fait accompli*—that there is no other possible way to address the Aha Epiphany about your industry than your compelling strategy.

How to Create Your One Big Idea

For some leaders, you will want to echo the thought leadership of the uppermost echelon in your organization. For other leaders, it will be more credible to quote the established or revered thought leader of your issue area or industry.

But for those of you who need to create your own thought leadership position, be ready to embrace chaos. So first, a warning for hyperanalytical, logical types: developing your thought leadership is not a linear path, but a circuitous one. If you love nice, neat formulas, this may be the most frustrating process for you. Thought leadership is an inspired act of creativity—taking disparate data sources, watching different trends, analyzing what you're seeing, and connecting unruly dots. It is driving to a breakthrough idea. An idea that inverts conventional wisdom. An idea that makes your audience's eyes widen with surprise, because it forces them to see the world in a different way.

What is that if not an echo of the creative process, the same one writers and scientists and artists and researchers use to create innovative work?

Let's develop your thought leadership story, knowing that the process will be messy, chaotic, and highly circuitous.

STEP ONE. Follow the thought leaders.

Make sure you are keeping abreast of analysts and futurists and provocateurs in your industry or issue area on social media. Follow them. Follow their links. Read whatever they're reading. Who are the thought leaders you need to follow?

_____

_____

_____

_____

_____

_____

_____

STEP TWO. Cross-reference material.

You'll start to see that thought leaders follow each other and that they comment on what each other is reading. Read everything. Then read some more. What materials are cited so repeatedly they need to move up on your must-read list?

_____

_____

_____

_____

_____

_____

_____

_____

_____

_____

STEP THREE. Test your initial insights with your own (safe) bubble first.

Share what you're seeing with your bubble: your leadership team, their direct reports, a few trusted people outside your organization. Are they seeing the same trends? Are they noticing other weak signals of change?

_____

_____

_____

_____

_____

_____

_____

_____

_____

_____

STEP FOUR. Rigorously assess the market trends.

Armed with the broader knowledge of what other thought leaders and your bubble are seeing, now's the perfect time to step back and assess the overall market trends with real, hard data.

- What's going on with the competition?

  _____

  _____

  _____

- How are customers changing?

  _____

  _____

  _____

- What do their changing demands and needs mean for the industry or issue area at large?

  _____

  _____

  _____

- Why is this urgent now?

  _____

  _____

  _____

- Why should we care?

  _____

  _____

  _____

- What will happen to our customers, our constituents, our world if the situation continues unchecked?

_____

_____

_____

STEP FIVE. Reflect on what's missing in the conversation.

You've spent some time reading. Now, take a step back and do some deep thinking. White boards help, particularly with people who you think are smarter than yourself.

- Given everything you've read and seen, what is your big aha insight?

_____

_____

_____

- Is anyone talking about that?

_____

_____

_____

- Where's the vacuum in the discussion?

_____

_____

_____

- What are people not talking about?

_____

_____

_____

- What are you adding that's new to the conversation?

_____

_____

_____

- Can you condense down to one pithy insight line?

_____

_____

_____

STEP SIX. Test your thought leadership in your own (safe) bubble.

Before you advance anything unique, much less incendiary, make sure you test your aha epiphany with your trusted advisors. Who are those trusted advisors?

_____

_____

_____

_____

_____

_____

_____

_____

STEP SEVEN. Refine your One Big Idea ... and then advance it with your best storytelling prowess.

How you share your thought leadership is just as important as developing your thought leadership. So here is a general framework for thinking about how to cue up your thought leadership in a speech.

Case Study: Thought Leadership

Let's take a look at how Gabrielle Fitzgerald, a former director at the Gates Foundation, advanced her One Big Idea on crafting global campaigns that can create lasting change.

"To do anything audacious—whether it's guaranteeing girls' education or eradicating polio itself—we can't do it alone. That's why I'm SO EXCITED to see a new trend in partnerships. We're moving from Grand Coalitions where you gather like-minded partners to Catalytic Coalitions where leaders in all sectors and societies UNITE their big voices and big resources around a big vision.

"They're global leaders. And active philanthropists. And private sector leaders.

"Some of these Catalytic Coalitions are made up of STRANGE BEDFELLOWS. Like: Raya the Muppet who likes to tell kids she wears her sandals everywhere … especially to the latrine. Or United Against Malaria, where partners ranged from superstar soccer players to Nando's Chicken.

"And increasingly, we're seeing more PHILANTHROPISTS join coalitions as true changemakers. These are the Mark Zuckerbergs and Bloombergs and Alito Dangotes who want to do more, not just fill in the gaps of funding. The philanthropists who want to fund science. And the ones who can rally their friends.

"The GREATEST moment in my career was at the Vaccine Summit where I saw the most unique gathering of leaders onstage: Traditional leaders and religious scholars shoulder-to-shoulder with CEOs of multinationals and NGOs. It was the Crown Prince of Abu Dhabi His Highness General Sheikh Mohammed bin Zayed bin Sultan Al Nahyan standing next to Sheika Lubna, Margaret Chan, Carlos Slim, Tony Blair, and Bill Gates.

FIRST: You may want to share one of your Defining Moments. Here's who I am as a leader and why I passionately care about this issue, cause, product, campaign.

SECOND: You introduce your Thought Leadership. Here's what I'm seeing from a big picture, and here's why it is important to all of us, our customers, our constituents, our planet.

THIRD: You tie that Thought Leadership into your Heritage and Quest. Here's what we as an organization have always stood for. Here is what we as an organization have always strived toward for our constituency.

FINALLY: With all the groundwork laid to establish belief in you as a leader and urgency as a unified team, now and only now do you share your Strategy and Plan. Now and only now do you talk about the actions you are asking your audience to take with you.

"This Catalytic Coalition used their unique skills and assets to provide children with low-cost, life-saving vaccines. What Catalytic Coalition are YOU building?"

Note the One Big Idea: We are moving away from Grand Coalitions of like-minded partners to Catalytic Coalitions of leaders in different sectors and societies.

Note how Gabrielle has simplified the big trends into digestible, understandable soundbites: These Catalytic Coalitions share big voices, big resources, and a big vision. They are made up of global leaders, active philanthropists, and private-sector leaders.

Note the storytelling embedded in the thought leadership: The Vaccine Summit with the most unique gathering of leaders onstage.

One Final Note on Thought Leadership

When you give a TED talk, you can focus 100 percent on the brilliance of your One Big Idea. But when you are leading an organization, your One Big Idea exists to galvanize support for your vision and strategy. Well-crafted thought leadership will convince your audience of the veracity, urgency, and strategic need for your plan. And it positions you as a big thinker, someone who commands a thorough understanding of your part of the world.

Thought Leadership is the portal to becoming a truly respected leader worth listening to ... and following.

PART THREE:
Storycraft

What is Storycraft?

"You need to create transcendent work!" exhorted Patti Lee Gauch, the legendary editor overseeing a writing retreat on one relentlessly gray November weekend. Twenty authors along with myself were gathered in a tiny port town north of Seattle to learn from the highly regarded former editorial director of a legendary New York publishing house. Patti has worked with some of the most storied names in children's literature—Eric Carle of *The Very Hungry Caterpillar* to Brian Jacques of the Red Wall series.

Four-foot-ten-inches or so of concentrated wisdom stood before us in her stockinged feet. Four-foot-ten-inches or so of conviction wielded a ruler as if that stick were a sword in her personal battle against lackluster prose.

"We need to know"—point!—"all the tools"—slash!—"in our toolkit." The ruler fell to Patti's side, but her challenge sizzled in the silent room. Our job as authors is to create stories that are utterly powerful, memorable, and full of truth. According to Patti, if we want to create not just good work, but transcendent work, then we must choose with surgical precision the tools to craft key moments in our novels.

This call for transcendence might be even more urgent for leaders. Leaders who rely on the emotional impact of stories to win donors' hearts and minds. Leaders who rely on their words—spoken and written—to communicate their vision, mission, and strategy. Leaders who rely on their fleet of employees and partners to turn that very vision into a plan, and that plan into action.

It is your job as a leader to know and use the best narrative and rhetorical tools at your disposal so you craft and give truly breakthrough and breathtaking speeches. So you speak with clarity and conviction. And so your audiences remember distinctly what you told them, and more than that, are so energized, they commit themselves to your strategy.

Try playing with these narrative tools in your next speech

- Intention
- Voice
- Metaphor
- Wordplay
- Magical objects

"People have forgotten how to tell a story. Stories don't have a middle or an end any more. They usually have a beginning that never stops beginning."

—*Steven Spielberg*

Intention

What is Intention?

As early as the third century BC, calligraphers in ancient China relied on inksticks and inkstones for their craft. Before a writing day, the calligrapher would take an inkstick and grind it against an inkstone, turning the ink into powder. Adding a droplet of water would turn that powder into usable ink. As Amy Tan wrote in *The Bonesetter's Daughter,* "That is the problem with modern ink from a bottle. You do not have to think. You simply write what is swimming on the top of your brain. And the top is nothing but pond scum, dead leaves, and mosquito spawn. But when you push an inkstick along an inkstone, you take the first step to cleansing your mind and your heart. You push and you ask yourself, 'What are my intentions? What is in my heart that matches my mind?'"

How we want our audience to feel—inspired or sobered, united or empowered—impacts everything: the stories that we share, the tone and tenor of the speech, the words that are used ... down to the color palette and imagery of the PowerPoint. In other words, the way we craft any executive communications is completely dependent on Intention.

> Before I begin to work on any speech for any executive, I make sure that the leader and I are absolutely clear about our Intention. Specifically, we ask ourselves, *What do we want the audience to feel, think, and do?* And we analyze it in exactly that order, because we know that if we can win people's hearts (feel), then it's much easier to convince them of the strategy (think) and actions (do).

Quick Assessment

Specifically, ask yourself these two questions:

- Who am I telling my story to?
- What do I want them to FEEL, THINK, DO?

Homework

So take a moment before you begin to work on your next major speech or webcast or email—and consider your intentions.

Voice

What is Voice?

When editors first read a manuscript, they are typically reading for "voice." They might scan the first two or three paragraphs, perhaps even the entire first chapter, with one question: Does the narrator have a resonant, authentic voice? Does the written word sound like a real person speaking in a compelling, I'm-telling-you-a-story tone?

From a corporate standpoint, "cost-efficient, user-friendly, community-driven" jargon is humanoid, not human. There is nothing uplifting about that so-called language, and if your intention is to inspire, then you as a leader must sound authentically like yourself in your voice. Not like a robot. Not like your speechwriter. Not even the way you think your favorite leader sounds. But you, the best version of you.

There are two voices that leaders need to unearth within themselves and deliver onstage: Personal Voice and Presidential Voice. It's the intertwining of the two that makes for the most resonant and authentic voice. And that is the **Leadership Voice**.

Personal Voice: This is what you hear when people talk about something that they are truly passionate about. All of a sudden, they are fully engaged. Their eyes glint. Their speaking voice warms up. To paraphrase Bill Drayton, the changemaker who coined the term "social entrepreneur," "Ask your leader about their passion—whether it's building, restoring, reading, skiing—and you will hear the magic." That magic is authentic, engaged, and personal voice.

Presidential Voice: Think of this as much more leaderly in tone. It's the voice of the expert talking about her area of expertise. It is the authoritative tone that commands respect just through the way your words are written or spoken.

To better understand this, watch the last State of the Union address or two. Whenever the President shares a personal story, listen to how Personal Voice is conversational, warm. The Personal Voice communicates: You would want to hang out with me. But whenever the President speaks about policy, the voice rings with authority. That Presidential Voice communicates: I know what I'm talking about. Notice that highly inspirational leaders move fluidly between Personal Voice and Presidential Voice.

Weaving together your Personal and Presidential voices makes you, as a leader, sound more:

authentic—AND authoritative.
conversational—AND credible.
down-to-earth—AND decisive.

How to Find Your Leadership Voice

Let's do some voice lessons to find your Leadership Voice, using your Defining Moment story, which you crafted in Part Two.

STEP ONE: Intention setting.

Spend a moment thinking about your intention in telling the story. You might find it easier to work with your communications expert, if you have one.

- Who is my audience?

  _____

  _____

  _____

- By my very last word, what do I want my audience to feel, think, and do?

  _____

  _____

  _____

STEP TWO: Analyzing your Defining Moment story.

Now that you know your intention for sharing your story, think about how you might be able to use your Defining Moment story to underscore your greater message (what you want the audience to *think*). What is the organizational relevance of your story? And if the Defining Moment story you created in Part Two doesn't land that point, then look into your arsenal of personal stories. Can you find another story within yourself that will help you make your point?

_____

_____

_____

_____

_____

_____

STEP THREE. Using your Personal Voice.

Reread the Defining Moment story that you wrote in Part Two. Set aside what you wrote, and imagine yourself sharing that same story with your best friend. Really, picture your best friend. Now, aloud, tell the story. Then tell it again as if you're sharing it with a grandparent.

- What words did you use to tell the story verbally that you didn't use in the written story?

  _____

  _____

  _____

- Did the way you shared the story sound more like you than the written word?

  _____

  _____

  _____

STEP FOUR. Rewriting in Personal Voice.

Now capture the words from that more conversational spoken story. Do not allow your industry jargon to creep in. If you find yourself aching to insert an acronym no one outside your team or industry or issue area would know, stop yourself. In fact, banish any word that you would never actually use in a conversation. This specifically includes polysyllabic vocabulary that might be fine in an academic journal and make you sound as if your IQ has suddenly jumped by twenty-five points. But you are not an audiobook for a three-inch thick textbook any more than you are for a marketing brochure.

_____

_____

_____

_____

_____

_____

STEP FIVE. Layering in Presidential Voice.

The preamble before your Defining Moment story and the insight line immediately after your story will be told in Presidential Voice.

Think of the preamble as the setup for the business relevance of your story. Every word should ring with conviction as befits a leader. Think of the insight line as the wisdom that you, as a leader, are imparting on your audience.

For instance, in a graduation speech at the University of North Carolina, an executive at the Gates Foundation shared her Defining Moment story, a story she had never told an audience. Here's an excerpt from this speech. Note the interplay between Presidential Voice to set up and close out the personal narrative and Personal Voice when she's sharing her story:

PRESIDENTIAL VOICE: "The moment I read the description of an MPH (Masters of Public Health) program—something to the effect of interdisciplinary solutions to improve the health of individuals and communities—I KNEW that this was what I. Was. Meant. To. Do.

PERSONAL VOICE: "I heard a whisper that said, *This is me.* That was so reassuring because it confirmed what I've wanted to do with my life since I was seventeen. That was the year my god-sister died of a brain tumor."

(Note: the leader went unscripted at this point to share the poignant story of her god-sister's death. She courageously talked about the ravages of radiation: the burned skin, the hair loss. Her voice, as you might expect, softened in tone. She sounded intimate as if she were conversing with good friends, albeit a couple of thousand good friends in the auditorium.)

PRESIDENTIAL VOICE: "That's why I hate—yes, HATE when life is taken WAY too quickly and WAY too soon. And that's why, from an early age I knew I had to ONE, give voice to those who don't have one when they need it most. And TWO, to protect people as much as possible from sickness and death through prevention."

Through the entwining of Presidential and Personal Voice, we can hear this changemaker's Leadership Voice: She sounds like an expert in her field, yet is approachable and authentic. And through the entire speech, we hear the undercurrent of personal passion that is her Leadership Voice.

So ask yourself:

- Where do you need to sound presidential in tone and words to establish yourself as an authority in your area?

- Are you using Presidential Voice to communicate information, insight, and thought leadership? Personal Voice to relay your personal stories?

STEP SIX. Reread your piece aloud.

If your story still doesn't sound like a real person—namely, you—then set aside your writing and record yourself telling the defining moment aloud. Literally, record yourself. Now, write down the words you used. That should sound Personal.

Now, focus in on the impact line—that last line that makes the story business relevant. Does that sound Presidential?

_____

_____

_____

_____

_____

_____

STEP SEVEN. Analyzing for Leadership Voice.

You might want to share your revised story with a few trusted advisors. Have them tell you honestly: does the Personal Voice sound like you? Why or why not? Does the Presidential Voice communicate expertise? Do you stay too long in one or another voice? Do you sound like a Leader worth following?

Coaching for Leadership Voice

Most leaders I've coached are exceptionally comfortable speaking in Presidential Voice. They know their industry or issue area better than anyone in any room. They can parse and quote data like the baseball statistician in *Moneyball*. They can speak authoritatively from the head of the boardroom table.

Yet speaking in Personal Voice is Uncomfortable. It's a little too revealing. A little too vulnerable. A little too weak.

Here's what I might suggest if you just cringed because you saw yourself in the above description.

In your next speech, challenge yourself to talk about your personal passion. Not a personal story, but a passion of yours. Perhaps you love to go geocaching. Or you've visited every single football stadium in Europe. Maybe you surf, golf, or do Ironman triathlons. Or you're a master gardener, sculptor, or antiques collector. Whatever your personal passion, insert it into the intro of your speech somehow. Your goal is to get yourself into that bright-eyed, engaged Personal Voice from the start purely as an experiment on storytelling.

Ask a trusted advisor to watch both you and the audience. Specifically ask them to assess:

- Did you build audience rapport faster than usual when you're onstage?
- Was your audience more attentive? More engaged? More relaxed?
- Were you yourself more engaging and relaxed?
- Were people texting—or otherwise being inattentive—while you shared your story versus the rest of your speech?

Trust me. I think you—and your audience—will be pleasantly surprised when you transform yourself into storyteller mode onstage.

Metaphor

What is a Metaphor?

If you want to boost your charisma, you should understand the research on presidential charisma. Inaugural speeches of Presidents in America deemed most charismatic used twice as many metaphors as the speeches of less-dynamic presidential leaders. Another study showed that when the best leaders realized that people weren't joining the vision, they used metaphors to paint a picture of what the vision would accomplish. And finally, neuroscience research suggests that people learn the best with a visual or verbal metaphor.

So what's a metaphor?

Let's scroll back to your elementary school days when you learned about figures of speech. A metaphor uses an object to symbolize another object, action, or idea.

For instance:

Music is the Viagra of creativity. (Okay, okay. Perhaps you will never be able to utter that particular metaphor onstage, but you get the point, yes? Metaphors can be cheeky, creative and effective. And that will only increase the likelihood of your message being remembered and repeated.)

Dona is the Nobel scientist of our company, always testing, testing, and testing until she drives to a startling breakthrough.

This product is the triathlete of technology: it is indestructible under water, its processor cycles twice as quickly as anything on the market, and it runs calculations wicked fast,

Since we know that people understand complex information when it's distilled into a metaphor, ask yourself:

What part of the strategy isn't your team understanding? Can you translate it for them in terms of a metaphor?

What is your favorite sport or hobby? Can you draw from that pursuit to craft a metaphor that resonates with you personally in a way that you can deliver it with conviction?

For instance: "So when I was in high school, I got to watch the Tour de France in person and witness The Power of the Peloton. That's the main group of riders who are up to 40 percent more efficient when they ride close to each other. We need to invest in our teams *so we are a peloton,* able to move together as one."

Coaching For The Metaphor Blocked

So you have a major case of writer's block and can't think of a metaphor. Then let's try using Rumi's metaphor-filled quote as a template, and you customize it to describe yourself as a leader.

> "Be a lamp, or a lifeboat, or a ladder. Help someone's soul heal. Walk out of your house like a shepherd."
>
> *—Rumi*

Your turn. What are you as a leader? Are you a lamp, lighting the way? Are you a lifeboat for your customers? Are you a ladder, helping your peers and team become better?

Here's an example that one leader used in a speech: "My purpose as a leader is to make sure this organization is ready for the future by being a BRIDGE to help us cross over obstacles, a MIRROR to help us see ourselves more clearly, and a CANARY to try out the air in new processes to make sure they're safe for you."

"Wit is the sudden marriage of ideas which, before their union, were not perceived to have any relation."

—*Mark Twain*

Wordplay

What is Tweet-Worthy Wordplay?

Being quoted by other executives, your peers, and your world is an important step in being seen as leader. Why? "Power lies in the leader who's able to distill complexity down to a single sound bite," says Vicki Lostetter, who has run talent development for divisions of Coca-Cola and Microsoft.

Creating a tweet-worthy sound bite is the surest way to be quoted. Naming and claiming a catchphrase is the antithesis of stultifying, bland, and indecipherable corporate-speak. So instead, unleash your creativity, play with words, and coin terms, such as "Tiger Mom," to describe the hyper-strict mother who makes it her life's mission to shape her child into a success, academically and professionally. Or "tamahagane grit" to communicate the type of resilience that the very best leaders exhibit, forged through extraordinarily difficult situations and circumstances.

Here are a few techniques to create your tweet-worthy sound bite

- **Use an apt metaphor.** (See the chapter on Metaphor.) For instance, you could say, "We employ some of the world's best researchers." Or you could say, "We send our own Neil Armstrongs—ethnographers and linguists, biologists and chemists—to make the unknown known in technology."

- **Use the Power of Three.** Our ears love lists of threes. Cue Shakespeare: "Friends, Romans, countrymen." Also, note that in this example, our ears enjoy the lyrical cadence of a phrase that are arranged from shortest to longest. So are there three items or concepts that you can list briefly that sound resonant to your ear?

- **Repeat, repeat, repeat.** Using the same phrase at the beginning of a succession of sentences adds rhythm. Case in point: in Dr. Martin Luther King, Jr.'s landmark speech, one entire section includes the stirring drumbeat of a phrase: "I have a dream..." Eight times in a row, Dr. King repeated that ringing phrase that has become immortal. And that is how he turned his dream into our dream.

- **Alliteration is your friend.** Again, our ears are attuned to the lyricism of alliteration. For instance, you could say, "We need people to believe that we're creative!" Or you could say, "We need to be seen as more than credible, but creative. More than believable, but beloved. More than trusted, but treasured."

Magical Objects

What are Magical Objects?

Look around your office. What do you have on display? Photos of the special people in your life? Mementos from a product launch, a successful campaign? A piece of art that reminds you of your favorite place on the planet? A letter from a world leader? These objects—or artifacts—hold special meaning and emotional significance beyond the items themselves. They are what writers sometimes call magical objects. J.R.R. Tolkien writes about the layered importance of these objects in his essay, *Tree and Leaf*. When you think about protagonists in stories, they often possess an object that holds significant meaning or represents their quest. Take the Ring for Frodo, or the Sword of Gryffindor for Harry Potter. Consider all the stolen books in *The Book Thief*. And the mockingjay pin in *The Hunger Games*. Think of Indiana Jones and his fedora. The letters in *Pride and Prejudice*.

Objects are just as important in your storytelling as a leader—and are woefully underused. But look at how impactful they can be. Remember how Alan Mulally, former CEO of Ford, scoured the company archives to search for his company's soul and found it in one of its first ad campaigns. That ad? Magical object. Think of those iconic Mickey Mouse ears for Disney. Or the secret formula for Coca-Cola. Magical objects.

For many pediatric hospitals, a special bell hangs silently on the wall. Only when a cancer patient finishes treatment does he or she get to ring the bell. Loudly. That bell marks the child's move from patient to survivor. That bell? You better believe it's a powerful magical object that signifies the relentless quest to cure children, the commitment of every doctor and nurse and staff to the care of the child, and the determination of the children themselves. The bell is a symbol of collective triumph.

So find the magical object that symbolizes your company, your project, or your campaign, and deploy it deliberately in your storytelling.

What magical object symbolizes your company and its quest? Yourself as a leader? Your project? Your campaign?

Is there a key moment when you can bring out that magical object in a tough meeting or important speech where you have to unify your leaders? Invigorate your employees? Convince your investors?

PART FOUR:
Putting It All Together

Putting It All Together

When you think about architecting your future speeches and other communications, both internal and external, consider this general structure:

FIRST:
Share your defining moment story and win people's hearts.

NEXT:
Share your thought leadership and win people's minds.

FINALLY:
Share your heritage, quest, and strategy to win people's feet.

Do this and your constituents will want to turn your vision into action.

The Keys to Inspiration

- [ ] Are you absolutely clear about your INTENTION? Do you know what you want your audience to feel, think, and do?

- [ ] Have you included your heritage and quest story? Your save-the-cat defining moment? Your lightning rod of thought leadership?

- [ ] Are you using both your Personal and Presidential Voices, weaving artfully between the two to speak in your Leadership Voice? Or do you sound monotone since you've stayed in Presidential Voice for too long?

- [ ] Have you created at least one metaphor to underscore your most important or most contentious point?

- [ ] Have you coined a term that aptly captures one of your main points? One that is tweet-worthy?

- [ ] Have you used a magical object to remind people of the importance of this quest?

"Practice isn't the thing you do once you're good. It's the thing you do that makes you good."

—Malcolm Gladwell, *Outliers: The Story of Success*

Rehearsal

Just Say Yes to Rehearsal

Do you want to hear pure exasperation? Then talk to your communications manager who can say this about you: "My exec won't rehearse."

Oh, really?

Do you want to know why Steve Jobs was consistently good onstage? He practiced. Not just once or twice. But legend has it, up to twelve times. And it showed in his ease and fluidity when he took the stage.

And Jimmy Fallon? Well, he rehearses in front of a test audience so he and his other writers know what jokes are flopping before they tape.

And all of those TED talk speakers? They have all rehearsed. Practice is part of the TED way.

An exceedingly few people can clamber onstage and deliver a speech flawlessly on their first try. Trust me on this. You don't want to be hunting for words when you're already nervous with the bright lights on you and the audience staring at you.

So rehearse.

And rehearse again.

Do your audience a favor and pay respect to your team whose work you are representing onstage: Rehearse.

Coaching For Stage Presence

Stage presence has so much to do with the right intonation. In speechwriting, I make sure that the words I want emphasized when spoken aloud are formatted in CAPS. And the pauses are noted through the opportune use of periods to separate key phrases. Even though the capitalization and punctuation are nonstandard for print, they work better when spoken.

Read the below excerpt aloud, making sure to put the emphasis on the words in CAPS. And to pause at the ellipses ... and periods.

"We are SO lucky that Bill and Melinda are great ADVOCATES for the issues they care about. Because of WHO they are. And WHAT they stand for. And HOW they work, our Gates Foundation brand is pretty well known. My hope (pause) is that we deploy our brand to HELP our partners to achieve THEIR goals."

Deliberate intonation helps prevent the deadly monotone that makes every speech feel three times as long as it really is.

Plus, using intonation will make you sound like a confident and poised leader, someone who is a delight to listen to and watch onstage. Someone who is presidential.

The Last Word

There is a saying among novelists: No tears from the writer, no tears from the reader. Certainly, there is a corollary for executive communications: No passion in the speechwriter, no passion in the speech giver.

Creating inspirational communications is a partnership between you and your communications expert, if you have one. As one executive noted, think of yourselves as the Avengers. Your superpower is leading. You bring your values. Your business acumen. Your insight. And your communicator's superpower is storycraft.

So please make yourself available. Please invite your communicator or another trusted advisor to important meetings. By all means, please flow critical information so your storytelling partner can supply you with the right stories that engage your employees, rally your funders, and jolt your constituents into action. To do this, as a senior leader with no time, you must partner with a storyteller whom you TRUST at a very personal level—both from a confidentiality and discretion standpoint.

Find one now. Because. Our world sorely needs better leaders.

As Steven Pressfield wrote in *The War of Art,* "Creative work is a gift to the world and every being in it. Don't cheat us of your contribution. Give us what you've got!"

Make no mistake. You have been given a gift: leadership. The very act of leading is intensely creative work with ever-changing scenes and circumstances.

Authentic, extraordinary leadership is a gift to the world and every single being in it.

Say YES to being the most extraordinary Chief Inspiration Officer you are meant to be.

Say YES to telling your organization's heritage and quest story, your own tamahagane-grit Defining Moment, and your One Big Idea thought leadership story.

Say YES to the world that is waiting to connect with you.

Now, get out there and lead your very best story!

Resources

Open Letter to Leaders, Changemakers, and Powers That Be

Originally published on The Rockefeller Foundation's storytelling site for social good: www.hatchforgood.org

Ed Catmull, *Creativity, Inc.: Overcoming the Unseen Forces That Stand in the Way of True Inspiration* (Random House, 2014).

Top Ten Traits of Extraordinary Leaders

Jim Collins and Morten T. Hansen, *Great by Choice* (New York: HarperBusiness, 2011).

Peter Ferdinand Drucker, Daniel Goleman, and Bill George, *HBR's 10 Must Reads on Leadership* (Harvard Business Review Press, 2011).

Carol Dweck, *Mindset: The New Psychology of Success* (Ballantine Books, 2007).

Part One: The Power of Story

Rich Karlgaard, *The Soft Edge: Where Great Companies Find Lasting Success* (Jossey-Bass, 2014).

Howard Gardner, *Leading Minds: An Anatomy of Leadership* (Basic Books, 2011).

Simon Sinek, TED Talk, "How Great Leaders Inspire Action."

John Medina, *Brain Rules: 12 Principles for Surviving and Thriving at Work, Home, and School* (Pear Press, 2014).

Peter Ferdinand Drucker, Daniel Goleman, and Bill George, *HBR's 10 Must Reads on Leadership* (Harvard Business Review Press, 2011).

Mayo Clinic, "A Prom Promise Kept," http://sharing.mayoclinic.org/discussion/a-prom-promise-kept

Part Two: The Leader's Stories

Bryce Hoffman, *American Icon: Alan Mulally and the Fight to Save Ford Motor Company* (Crown Business, 2013).

Joseph Campbell, *The Hero with a Thousand Faces* (New World Library, 2008).

Blake Snyder, *Save the Cat* (Michael Wiese Productions, 2005).

Brené Brown, TED Talk, "The Power of Vulnerability."

Steve Jobs, Stanford Commencement speech, 2005.

Part Three: Storycraft

Patricia Lee Gauch, http://patricialeegauch.com

Amy Tan, *The Bonesetter's Daughter* (Ballantine Books, 2003).

Jeffrey Mio, Ronald Riggio, Shana Levin, Renford Reese, "Presidential leadership and charisma: The effects of metaphor," http://cognitivepolitics.ucr.edu/events/mio/mio_etal_2005.pdf

J.R.R. Tolkien, *Tree and Leaf: Including Mythopoeia* (HarperCollins, 2012).

Putting It All Together

Malcolm Gladwell, *Outliers: The Story of Success* (Back Bay Books, 2011).

Steven Pressfield, *The War of Art: Break Through the Blocks and Win Your Inner Creative Battles* (Black Irish Entertainment, 2012).

ACKNOWLEDGMENTS

Deepest gratitude to The Rockefeller Foundation—notably Neill Coleman, Jay Geneske, and Traci Carpenter. This book was inspired during the many rich discussions at our Storytelling for Social Good convening, led by the inimitable Spitfire Strategies. Seriously, if you want to witness Spitfires who lead with integrity and wit, you must behold Kristen Grimm and Ellie Klerlein in action.

As well, I'd like to honor all of my executive clients who have taught me the true meaning of grit, risk-taking, vulnerability, leadership, and storytelling. Most especially, I want to thank Sue Bevington, Gabrielle Fitzgerald, and Nicole Bates for allowing me to share their words. So grateful for my early readers: Meg Lippert, Jackie Parker-Robinson, Kathleen March, and Darcy Brixey. No words can express my thanks for Martha Brockenbrough who trained her expert editorial eye on the manuscript. And Robert Coronado for his exceptional design skills.

Special thanks to my agent, Steven Malk, and my business partner, Deb Cragen—both of whom sustain me with their steadfast belief and support. Robbie Bach who nudged me with gentle persistence for years to write this book. And as always, Tyler and Sofia who inspire me every single day.

About The Author

Storytelling runs in Justina Chen's blood. After all, her middle name—Yi-Yen—means illuminate, which is what story does: it throws light on a message.

Justina is a story strategist, trusted communications advisor to leaders, and an award-winning novelist. She has worked for numerous presidents at Microsoft, where her work was lauded for "almost single-handedly changing the way we think about executive communications at Microsoft. Her work has been a staggering reminder of the power of exquisite storytelling."

Her executive storytelling draws from her work in PR, marketing, and as an award-winning novelist for teens. Her most recent book, A *Blind Spot for Boys,* is on a Booklist Top 10 list. *North of Beautiful* was named one of the Best Books of the Year by Kirkus Reviews and was a finalist of nine state book awards. And her debut novel, *Nothing but the Truth (and a few white lies),* won the Asian-American Award for Literature.

A passionate advocate of literacy, Justina co-founded readergirlz, a cutting-edge social media project for teens, which won the National Book Foundation's Prize for Innovations in Reading. She graduated Phi Beta Kappa from Stanford University with honors in Economics.

She's called Sydney and Shanghai home, and currently lives in Seattle with her two kids. Even so, she feels at ease wherever she goes so long as she has her coconut black tea, journal, and pen.

SHARE YOUR STORY WITH ME

Twitter: @justinaychen

Web: www.justinachen.com

Seminar: www.upstartleader.com